Gymnastics Conditioning, Fitness Training for the Gymnast

Karen M. Goeller

www.GymnasticsBooks.com

Most of our books are available at quantity discounts. For information please write to the author and publisher. Contact information can be found through the website, GymnasticsBooks.com.

ISBN: 978-0-6151-4759-8

Gymnastics Conditioning, Fitness Training for the Gymnast

It is important that a gymnast maintain a certain fitness level in order to allow her to compete safely in the sport. She must maintain a high enough fitness level to help prevent injury and progress through the gymnastics levels efficiently.

A gymnast must be on a much higher fitness level than those people not participating in competitive sports. It is for that reason a gymnast must spend a great deal of their time performing strength, endurance, and flexibility exercises, among others, as part of their training. The workouts must include general strength exercises as well as sport specific exercises. This balance can often be difficult to achieve correctly when a new coach or gymnast begins to organize a gymnastics training program.

The workouts created in this book instruct the gymnast to perform both general strength and sport specific conditioning within one workout. They will not only help by teaching several new conditioning workouts, but they will help the coach or gymnast learn to develop workouts on their own which will lead to a more well rounded training program and therefore a stronger, more conditioned gymnast!

Contents

Endurance and Low Body Conditioning

Sets	Reps	Weight/Resistance	Tempo	Time
1				20 sec

Balance Board Drill
1. Start by standing on the balance board allowing one side to touch the ground.
2. Slightly bend your knees with a shoulder width stance.
3. Using the muscles in the lower leg raise the board edge off the ground so that you are balancing on the fulcrum.
4. Hold for the prescribed time.

Additional Comments
Allow the board to rock forward and back several times before holding the balance. This is to help warm up and condition your athletes ankles and lower body.

	Sets	Reps	Weight/Resistance	Tempo	Time
	1	15 Right			
	2	15 Left			

Hip Flexor Thrust
1. Stand with feet hip width apart and place a band around the ankle. The band should be fixed to an object at the other end.
2. Raise the leg that has the band forward and hip. Think of driving your knee out and then up towards the ceiling.
3. Tighten your core and maintain balance when performing this exercise.
4. Return to the starting position and repeat. Perform with the other leg.

Additional Comments
This exercise should help warm up your athletes hip flexors. Make sure you warn your athletes that bands occasionally break.

Sets	Reps	Weight/Resistance	Tempo	Time

Bounding / Deer Runs
1. Jog into the start of the drill for forward momentum.
2. After a few feet, forcefully push off with the left foot and bring the leg forward. At same time drive your right arm forward.
3. Repeat with other leg and arm.
4. This exercise is an exaggerated running motion focusing on foot push-off and air time.

Additional Comments
Set up this and the next four exercises so that the athletes can move through them as a short obstacle course. Instruct your athletes to alternate this and the next four exercises for 1 - 3 minutes. Make sure they do not stop in between exercises unless they feel dizzy, nauseous, ill, or injured.

Gymnastics Conditioning, Fitness Training
for the Gymnast

	Sets	Reps	Weight/Resistance	Tempo	Time

Hurdle Jumps
1. Stand 1-2 feet away from hurdle. Feet should be slightly wider than hip-width apart in a semi-squat position.
2. Driving the arms up and jump over hurdle.
3. Upon landing, quickly jump over next hurdle.

Additional Comments
You can use pit cubes or other small objects for your gymnasts to jump over. Remind them to rebound rather than stopping between each hurdle.
Move onto Two Foot Zig Zag immediately.

Sets	Reps	Weight/Resistance	Tempo	Time
1	15			

Two Foot Zig Zap Hops

1. Stand to the left of the ladder approximately 1-2 feet away.
2. Forcefully push off both feet and land the on the other side of the ladder.
3. Repeat and land feet back on the other side, continue repeating and so on down the ladder.
4. Do not "double hop" upon each landing.

Additional Comments

You can use any line on the floor exercise area. The best product for this exercise is the Vinyl Beam found at GymnasticsStuff.com.
Move onto Lateral Barrier Jump immediately.

	Sets	Reps	Weight/Resistance	Tempo	Time
	1	15			

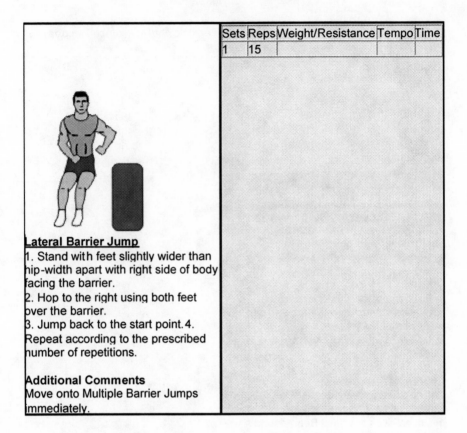

Lateral Barrier Jump

1. Stand with feet slightly wider than hip-width apart with right side of body facing the barrier.
2. Hop to the right using both feet over the barrier.
3. Jump back to the start point. 4. Repeat according to the prescribed number of repetitions.

Additional Comments
Move onto Multiple Barrier Jumps immediately.

Sets	Reps	Weight/Resistance	Tempo	Time

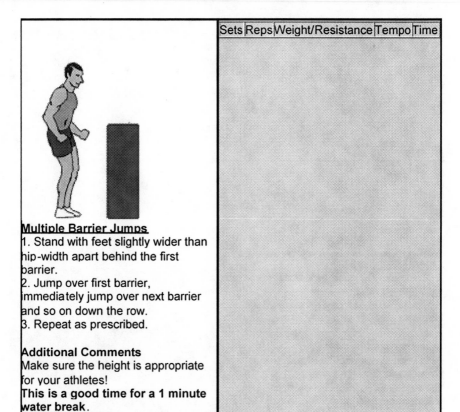

Multiple Barrier Jumps
1. Stand with feet slightly wider than hip-width apart behind the first barrier.
2. Jump over first barrier, immediately jump over next barrier and so on down the row.
3. Repeat as prescribed.

Additional Comments
Make sure the height is appropriate for your athletes!
This is a good time for a 1 minute water break.

	Sets	Reps	Weight/Resistance	Tempo	Time
	1	15 Right			
	2	15 Left			

Lateral High Hops
1. Stand to left side of box and place right foot on top of box.
2. Push off the box using the right leg only and explode vertically as high as possible. Drive the arms forward and up for maximum height.
3. Land with opposite foot onto box. Repeat with the other foot.
4. Repeat according to prescribed number of repetitions.

Additional Comments
Remind your athletes to continue moving until they reach 15 with each leg. Set up this and the next few exercises if you have not already done so. Once your athletes have completed 15 lateral High Hops they should move onto the Jump and Land on BOSU.

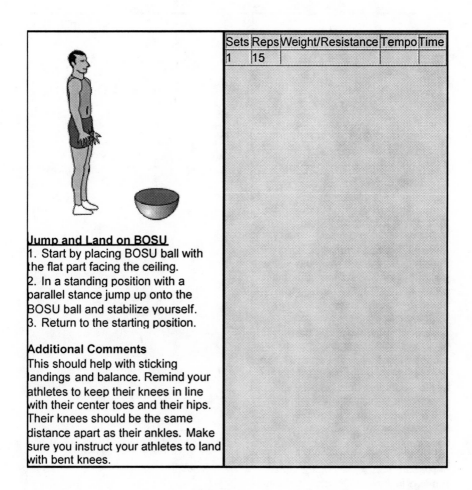

Sets	Reps	Weight/Resistance	Tempo	Time
1	15			

Jump and Land on BOSU
1. Start by placing BOSU ball with the flat part facing the ceiling.
2. In a standing position with a parallel stance jump up onto the BOSU ball and stabilize yourself.
3. Return to the starting position.

Additional Comments
This should help with sticking landings and balance. Remind your athletes to keep their knees in line with their center toes and their hips. Their knees should be the same distance apart as their ankles. Make sure you instruct your athletes to land with bent knees.

Sets	Reps	Weight/Resistance	Tempo	Time
1	15 Right			
2	15 Left			

Stationary Lunge on BOSU

1. Stand with feet hip width apart. Take left leg and step back approximately 2 feet standing on the ball of the foot. Place the other ball on top of a BOSU ball or balance board and balance disc.
2. Start position: Feet should be positioned at a staggered stance with head and back erect and straight in a neutral position. Place hands on hips.
3. Lower body by bending at right hip and knee until thigh is parallel to floor. Body should follow a straight line down towards the floor.
4. Return to start position.

Additional Comments

Make sure your athlete's front knee remains in line with their center toe. Make sure their knee does not pass their toe. Instruct your athlete not to allow their back knee to touch the floor. Instruct your athlete to keep their chest up throughout the exercise.

Sets	Reps	Weight/Resistance	Tempo	Time
1	15 Right			
2	15 Left			

Plank Knee-ins
1. Start by getting on your hands and knees then lifting up to a push-up position.
2. Keeping your abs tight and your trunk parallel bring one knee in towards your chest.
3. Return the foot back to the starting position and repeat with the same leg.
4. Once all repetitions are completed with one leg perform this exercise with the other leg.

Additional Comments
Instruct your athlete not to allow their foot to touch the floor while bringing their knee toward their chest and while returning their foot back to the starting position. (Athlete will reach a tuck position with one leg.)

Sets	Reps	Weight/Resistance	Tempo	Time
1	15 Right			
2	15 Left			

Mountain Climbers
1. Start by getting on your hands and feet in a prone position. {Push-up position)
2. Keeping your body parallel to the floor, drive your knees up towards your chest alternating back and forth.
3. Repeat this movement for the required number of seconds.

Additional Comments
Inform your athletes that this is similar to running in place with their hands on the floor.

Endurance and Low Body Conditioning

Sets	Reps	Weight/Resistance	Tempo	Time
1	15 Right			
2	15 Left			

Pushup Superman w/ Alternating Arms
1. Starting Position: Start the movement in a plank position. (Push-up position)
2. Holding that position, raise your right arm and left leg off of the ground.
3. Return to the starting position and repeat with the other arm and leg. Hold each lift for 1-2 seconds.

Additional Comments
Instruct your athletes to perform this exercise with a nonstop motion. Instruct your athletes to perform this exercise with a constant motion. The arm lift will help condition the shoulders and should help with a cast handstand. The leg left will help condition the athlete's low back. Remaining in this position will help condition the athlete's core.

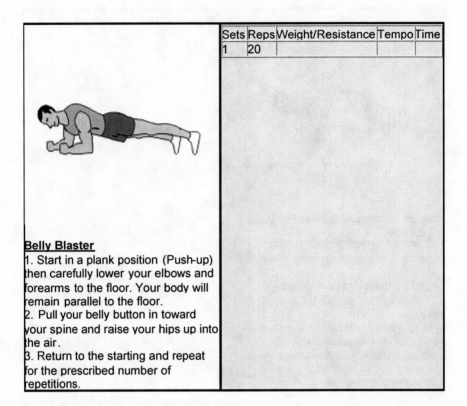

Sets	Reps	Weight/Resistance	Tempo	Time
1	20			

Belly Blaster
1. Start in a plank position (Push-up) then carefully lower your elbows and forearms to the floor. Your body will remain parallel to the floor.
2. Pull your belly button in toward your spine and raise your hips up into the air.
3. Return to the starting and repeat for the prescribed number of repetitions.

Sets	Reps	Weight/Resistance	Tempo	Time
1	20			

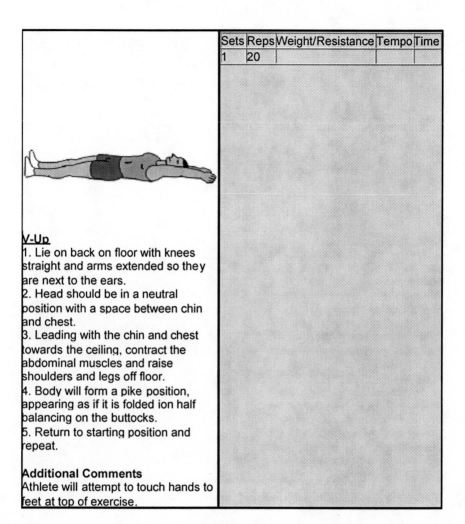

V-Up
1. Lie on back on floor with knees straight and arms extended so they are next to the ears.
2. Head should be in a neutral position with a space between chin and chest.
3. Leading with the chin and chest towards the ceiling, contract the abdominal muscles and raise shoulders and legs off floor.
4. Body will form a pike position, appearing as if it is folded ion half balancing on the buttocks.
5. Return to starting position and repeat.

Additional Comments
Athlete will attempt to touch hands to feet at top of exercise.

Sets	Reps	Weight/Resistance	Tempo	Time
1	20			

Reverse Crunch (Tuck)
1. Start by lying on your back with your hands behind or above your head.
2. Bend knees. Knees will remain bent throughout exercise.
3. Proceed to draw in your belly button toward your spine and lift both legs up at the same time towards your chest.
4. Once knees are lifted into chest as much as possible, the buttocks will slightly lift off the floor, making the athlete more round.
5. Return to the starting position and repeat making sure that you do not arch your back as you are lowering or raising your legs.

Sets	Reps	Weight/Resistance	Tempo	Time
1	20			

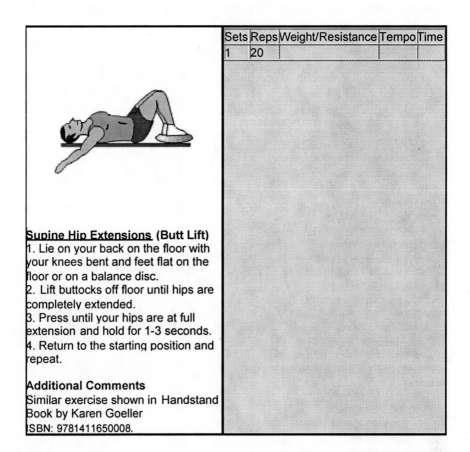

Supine Hip Extensions (Butt Lift)
1. Lie on your back on the floor with your knees bent and feet flat on the floor or on a balance disc.
2. Lift buttocks off floor until hips are completely extended.
3. Press until your hips are at full extension and hold for 1-3 seconds.
4. Return to the starting position and repeat.

Additional Comments
Similar exercise shown in Handstand Book by Karen Goeller
ISBN: 9781411650008.

Sets	Reps	Weight/Resistance	Tempo	Time
1	15 Right			
2	15 left			

Single Leg Hip Extension
1. Lie on your back on the floor with your knees bent and feet flat on the floor or on a balance disc.
2. Raise one foot off the balance disc and straighten that knee.
Keeping the knees together, lift buttocks off floor until hips are completely extended.
3. Press until your hips are at full extension and hold for 1-3 seconds.
4. Return to the starting position and repeat.

Additional Comments
Similar exercise shown in Handstand Book by Karen Goeller
ISBN: 9781411650008.

Sets	Reps	Weight/Resistance	Tempo	Time
1				20 sec
2				20 sec

Side Lying Quad Stretch
1. Lie on your left side on floor.
2. Pull heel of right leg toward buttocks until stretch is felt in front of right thigh.
3. Hold for 20-30 seconds.
4. Roll to other side and perform stretch on other leg.
5. Repeat stretch starting with right leg and finishing with left leg..

Additional Comments
Remember to keep the low back straight - avoid hyper extending back during stretch by keeping abdominals tight.

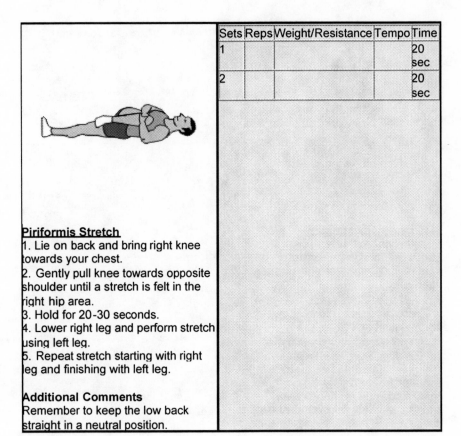

Sets	Reps	Weight/Resistance	Tempo	Time
1				20 sec
2				20 sec

Piriformis Stretch
1. Lie on back and bring right knee towards your chest.
2. Gently pull knee towards opposite shoulder until a stretch is felt in the right hip area.
3. Hold for 20-30 seconds.
4. Lower right leg and perform stretch using left leg.
5. Repeat stretch starting with right leg and finishing with left leg.

Additional Comments
Remember to keep the low back straight in a neutral position.

Endurance and Low Body 2

Sets	Reps	Weight/ Resistance	Tempo	Time
1	15 Rocks			
2	Balance			15 seconds
3	15 Rocks			
4	Balance			15 seconds

Balance Board Drill
1. Start by standing on the balance board allowing one side to touch the ground.
2. Slightly bend your knees with a shoulder width stance.
3. Using the muscles in the lower leg raise the board edge off the floor so that you are balancing on the fulcrum.
4. Hold for the prescribed time.

Additional Comments
Tip the board forward and back, allowing the front edge to touch the floor and then the back edge to touch the floor. After 15 Rocks (Edge taps) balance for 15 seconds. Repeat the rocks and balance.

Sets	Reps	Weight/ Resistance	Tempo	Time
1	15 Rocks			
2	Balance			15 seconds
3	15 Rocks			
4	Balance			15 seconds

Single Leg Balance Board Drill

1. Start by standing on the balance board allowing one side to touch the ground.
2. Raise one foot off the board and slightly bend your knee of the planted foot.
3. Using the muscles in the lower leg raise the board edge off the ground so that you are balancing on the fulcrum.
4. Hold for the prescribed time and repeat with the other leg.

Additional Comments

Tip the board forward and back, allowing the front edge to touch the floor and then the back edge to touch the floor. After 15 Rocks (Edge taps) balance for 15 seconds. Repeat the rocks and balance.

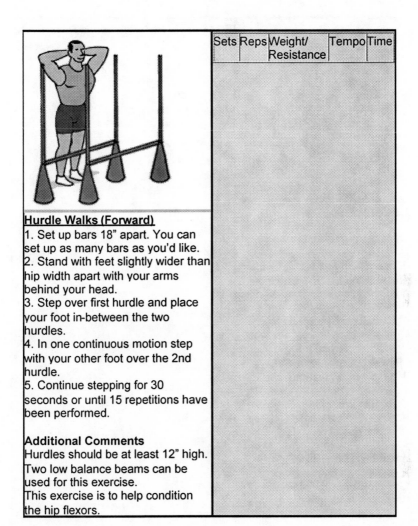

Sets	Reps	Weight/ Resistance	Tempo	Time

Hurdle Walks (Forward)
1. Set up bars 18" apart. You can set up as many bars as you'd like.
2. Stand with feet slightly wider than hip width apart with your arms behind your head.
3. Step over first hurdle and place your foot in-between the two hurdles.
4. In one continuous motion step with your other foot over the 2nd hurdle.
5. Continue stepping for 30 seconds or until 15 repetitions have been performed.

Additional Comments
Hurdles should be at least 12" high.
Two low balance beams can be used for this exercise.
This exercise is to help condition the hip flexors.

Sets	Reps	Weight/Resistance	Tempo	Time

Lateral Hurdle Walks

1. Set up bars 18" apart. You can set up as many bars as you'd like.
2. Stand with feet hip-width apart and with the bar to your left or right. Hands and arms should be behind your head.
3. Step over the bar with the closest foot to desired direction (left or right) using a feet together - feet apart motion.
4. Keep hips and shoulders squared throughout movement.
5. Repeat in opposite direction according to prescribed repetitions.

Additional Comments

Hurdles should be at least 12" high. Low balance beams can be used for this exercise.
This exercise is to help condition the hip flexors.

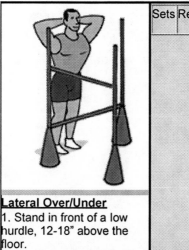

	Sets	Reps	Weight/ Resistance	Tempo	Time

Lateral Over/Under
1. Stand in front of a low hurdle, 12-18" above the floor.
2. With the left foot, perform a forward step over the low hurdle, shift weight to the left foot once placed on floor in front of hurdle.
3. Immediately upon shifting weight to the left leg, squat down into a crouched position. Immediately step to the right under the high hurdle. Over, under motion.
4. Return to the starting position and repeat with the opposite foot. Focus on quickness and fluid movement.

Additional Comments
It is a quick over under motion, lifting one leg over the first hurdle and then performing an immediate squat to move under the high hurdle.
A low balance beam and a high beam can be used.

	Sets	Reps	Weight/Resistance	Tempo	Time

Straight Leg Quick Feet

1. Run, tapping toes in front of body, keeping your legs straight, and feet pointed toward the ground in front of body.
2. Focus on minimizing ground contact with the foot and pull through with the leg.
3. Steps should be approximately one foot apart.

Additional Comments
Set up the area for this and the following exercises so that the athletes can move through them without interruption.
It is recommended that you use a soft surface in order to help prevent shin splints or other chronic pain.

Sets	Reps	Weight/ Resistance	Tempo	Time

High Knee Drill
1. Stand at foot of agility ladder or just stand in place.
2. Drive knee up towards chest and place that foot in first square or back on the ground.
3. Drive other knee up and land in next square and so on down the ladder in a moderate to fast jog with minimal ground contact time.
4. Knee should be lifted to belly button height with each step.

Additional Comments
Similar exercise found in the running section of the book, Gymnastics Drills and Conditioning Exercises."
ISBN: 9781411605794

	Sets	Reps	Weight/Resistance	Tempo	Time

Butt Kick
1. Start with a light jog
2. Pull the heel of the lower leg up to and bounce off the butt.
3. Immediately switch feet, moving forward, kicking buttocks with each step.

Additional Comments
Similar exercise found in the running section of the book, Gymnastics Drills and Conditioning Exercises."
ISBN: 9781411605794

Sets	Reps	Weight/ Resistance	Tempo	Time

Bounding / Deer Runs
1. Jog into the start of the drill for forward momentum.
2. After a few feet, forcefully push off with the left foot and bring the leg forward. At same time drive your right arm forward.
3. Repeat with other leg and arm.
4. This exercise is an exaggerated running motion focusing on foot push-off and air time.

Additional Comments
Make sure your athletes do not stop in between exercises unless they feel dizzy, nauseous, ill, or injured. Use the vault runway or the floor exercise area. It is recommended you use the softest surface available in order to help prevent shin splints or other chronic pain.

Similar exercise found in the running section of the book, Gymnastics Drills and Conditioning Exercises."
ISBN: 9781411605794

	Sets	Reps	Weight/Resistance	Tempo	Time

Skip

1. Start with both feet together and begin by driving your left leg up into the air and explode off the ground using the right ankle (like an explosive toe raise).

2. Extend the left leg out into an extended horizontal position and then lower the foot.

3. Immediately extend the right foot so that you land 1-2 feet in front of the starting position with the right foot landing.

4. Place left foot on the ground in a skipping motion and drive the right leg up and out while extending the left ankle in a skipping motion.

5. Continue skipping for at least 30 feet.

Additional Comments
Instruct your athletes to bend their knee as their foot returns to the floor.

Sets	Reps	Weight/ Resistance	Tempo	Time

Tuck Jump
1. Stand with feet shoulder-width apart, knees slightly bent, with arms at sides.
2. Jump up bringing knees up to chest.
3. Land on balls of feet and repeat immediately, as if tapping toes on floor
4. Remember to reduce ground contact time by landing soft on feet and springing into air.
These jumps can be performed traveling forward or in place.

Additional Comments
You can have your athletes perform the tuck jumps over cones or pit cubes.

Sets	Reps	Weight/Resistance	Tempo	Time
1	Left			
2	Right			

Single Leg Run Through
1. Start by setting up hurdles at a comfortable distance between them.
2. Start running and bring your left leg up and over the first hurdle.
3. Place it back on the ground and continue to run until the next hurdle and do the same step over with the left leg.
4. Continue running, lifting the inside leg over the hurdle for at least 30 feet.
5. Repeat exercise with the right leg will go over the hurdles.

Additional Comments
You can use cones or stack 2 pit cubes for this exercise.

Make sure your athletes use the other leg on the second round of this exercise. Left leg goes over hurdle while right leg is the outside leg then on the next turn the right leg uses the hurdle while the left leg is the outside leg.

Sets	Reps	Weight/ Resistance	Tempo	Time
1	15 Right			
2	15 Left			

Stationary Lunge on BOSU
1. Place the right foot on a BOSU Ball.
2. Take left leg and step back approximately 2 feet.
2. Feet should be positioned at a staggered stance with head and back upright and straight in a neutral position.
3. Place hands on hips.
4. Lower body by bending at right hip and knee until thigh is parallel to floor. Body should follow a straight line down towards the floor.
5. Return to start position.
6. Repeat with other leg.

Additional Comments
Make sure your athlete's front knee remains in line with their center toe. Make sure their knee does not pass their toe. Instruct your athlete not to allow their back knee to touch the floor. Instruct your athlete to keep their chest up throughout the exercise.

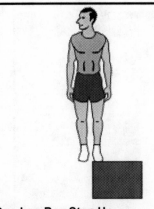

Sets	Reps	Weight/Resistance	Tempo	Time
1	15 Right			
2	15 Left			

One Leg Box Step Up
1. Stand in front of a box or folded mat. Make sure box is at or below knee height of athlete.
2. Place left foot on top of box.
3. Raise body using the muscles of the left leg until leg is nearly extended and you are on top of box. Right foot is not placed on top of box.
4. Lower to start position keeping the left foot on top of box.
5. Repeat Step Up with right leg according to exercise prescription.

Additional Comments
Make sure your athlete's front knee remains in line with their center toe. Make sure their knee does not pass their toe (go in front of their toe).

Sets	Reps	Weight/ Resistance	Tempo	Time
1	Right Leg			20 seconds
2	Left Leg			20 seconds

Standing Quad Stretch
1. Standing with a shoulder width stance and hold onto a sturdy object to help with balance.
2. Bring left foot up and grab with your hand.
3. Pull your left foot up until you feel a stretch on the front of your left thigh.
4. Hold for 20 seconds and repeat with the right leg.

Additional Comments
You can instruct our athletes to move into their normal stretching at this point. This is a good time for a 1 minute water break. Make sure your athletes stretch their hip flexors and hamstrings really well.

Warm Up – Before Stretch

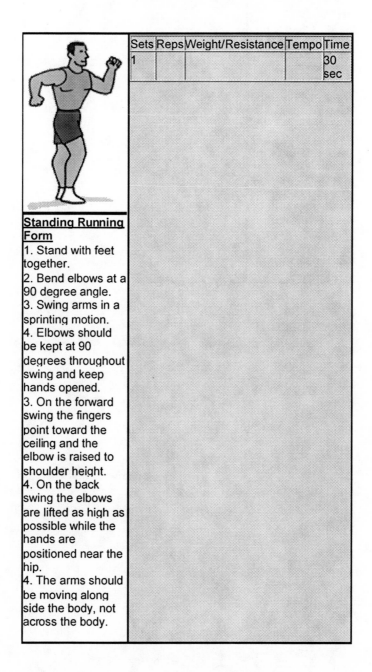

Sets	Reps	Weight/Resistance	Tempo	Time
1				30 sec

Standing Running Form

1. Stand with feet together.
2. Bend elbows at a 90 degree angle.
3. Swing arms in a sprinting motion.
4. Elbows should be kept at 90 degrees throughout swing and keep hands opened.
3. On the forward swing the fingers point toward the ceiling and the elbow is raised to shoulder height.
4. On the back swing the elbows are lifted as high as possible while the hands are positioned near the hip.
4. The arms should be moving along side the body, not across the body.

Gymnastics Conditioning, Fitness Training for the Gymnast

Additional Comments Make sure your athletes do not perform a karate chop motion while swinging their arms. Their arms remain bent at a 90 degree angle throughout the swing. Have your athletes move from one exercise to the next exercise as quickly as possible to help build endurance. Make sure they stop if they feel dizzy, nauseous, ill, or injured.	

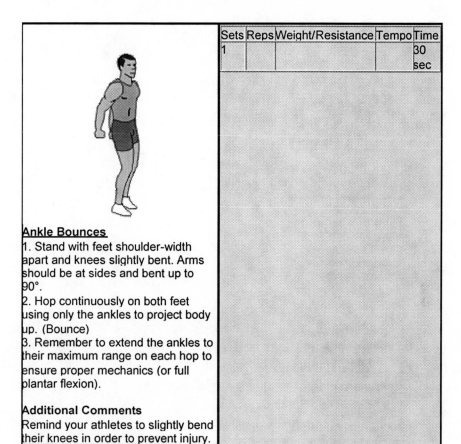

Sets	Reps	Weight/Resistance	Tempo	Time
1				30 sec

Ankle Bounces
1. Stand with feet shoulder-width apart and knees slightly bent. Arms should be at sides and bent up to 90°.
2. Hop continuously on both feet using only the ankles to project body up. (Bounce)
3. Remember to extend the ankles to their maximum range on each hop to ensure proper mechanics (or full plantar flexion).

Additional Comments
Remind your athletes to slightly bend their knees in order to prevent injury.

Sets	Reps	Weight/Resistance	Tempo	Time
1				30 sec

High Knee Drill
1. Stand at foot of agility ladder or just stand in place.
2. Drive knee up towards chest and place that foot in first square or back on the ground.
3. Drive other knee up and land in next square and so on down the ladder in a moderate to fast jog with minimal ground contact time.
4. Knee should be lifted to belly button height with each step.

Additional Comments
Similar exercise found in the running section of the book, Gymnastics Drills and Conditioning Exercises."
ISBN: 9781411605794

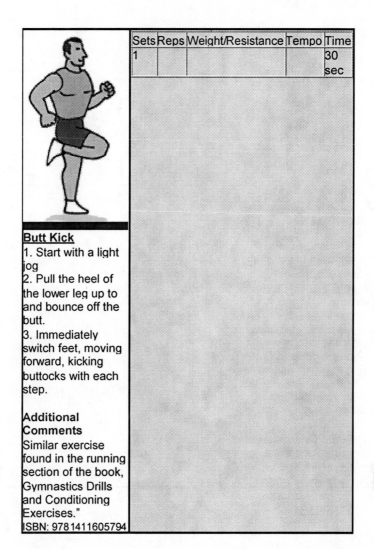

Sets	Reps	Weight/Resistance	Tempo	Time
1				30 sec

Butt Kick
1. Start with a light jog
2. Pull the heel of the lower leg up to and bounce off the butt.
3. Immediately switch feet, moving forward, kicking buttocks with each step.

Additional Comments
Similar exercise found in the running section of the book, Gymnastics Drills and Conditioning Exercises."
ISBN: 978 1411605794

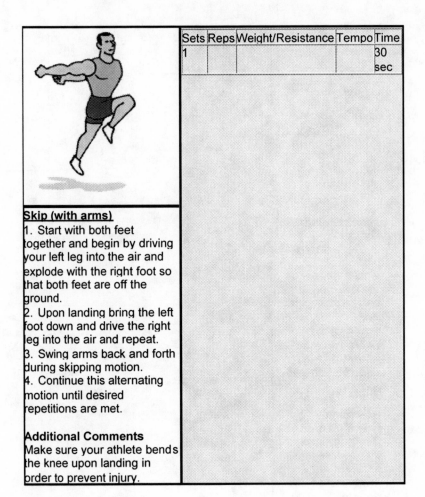

Sets	Reps	Weight/Resistance	Tempo	Time
1				30 sec

Skip (with arms)
1. Start with both feet together and begin by driving your left leg into the air and explode with the right foot so that both feet are off the ground.
2. Upon landing bring the left foot down and drive the right leg into the air and repeat.
3. Swing arms back and forth during skipping motion.
4. Continue this alternating motion until desired repetitions are met.

Additional Comments
Make sure your athlete bends the knee upon landing in order to prevent injury.

Sets	Reps	Weight/Resistance	Tempo	Time
1				30 sec

Power Jacks

1. Start in a shoulder width stance with your knees slightly bent.
2. Jump up into the air and spread your legs out into a wide stance and land in this position. (A straddle stand with bent knees.)
3. Immediately proceed into a squat and then stand back up into a jump to land with both feet at a shoulder width stance.
4. Repeat this movement for the recommended repetitions.

Additional Comments

These jumping jacks require a deeper knee bend on the wide leg portion as if performing a squat. Knees should remain in line with the center toe rather than fall in towards each other. Bend is at the knees and hips.

Sets	Reps	Weight/Resistance	Tempo	Time
1				15 sec R
2				15 sec L

Bodyweight Forward Lunge

1. Start by standing with your feet shoulder width apart.
2. Step forward with one foot and bend your knees into a lunge position.
3. Your back knee should come close to touching the ground and your front leg should be bent to about 90 degrees at the knee.
4. Maintain your upright posture throughout the movement.
5. Return to the starting position and repeat. Once repetitions are completed then repeat with the other leg.

Additional Comments

Have your athletes perform lunges with one leg at a time, 15 seconds each leg. Make sure their front knee remains in line with their center toe. Make sure their front knee does not go further forward than their toe. Instruct your athlete to keep their chest up throughout this exercise. Remind your athlete not to allow their back knee to touch the floor.

Sets	Reps	Weight/Resistance	Tempo	Time
1				30 sec

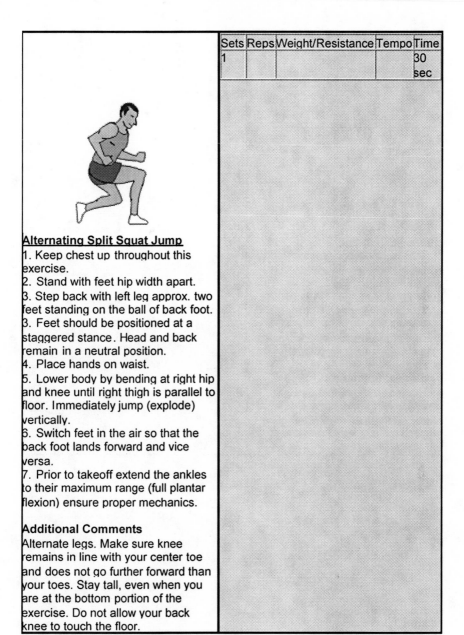

Alternating Split Squat Jump
1. Keep chest up throughout this exercise.
2. Stand with feet hip width apart.
3. Step back with left leg approx. two feet standing on the ball of back foot.
3. Feet should be positioned at a staggered stance. Head and back remain in a neutral position.
4. Place hands on waist.
5. Lower body by bending at right hip and knee until right thigh is parallel to floor. Immediately jump (explode) vertically.
6. Switch feet in the air so that the back foot lands forward and vice versa.
7. Prior to takeoff extend the ankles to their maximum range (full plantar flexion) ensure proper mechanics.

Additional Comments
Alternate legs. Make sure knee remains in line with your center toe and does not go further forward than your toes. Stay tall, even when you are at the bottom portion of the exercise. Do not allow your back knee to touch the floor.

Sets	Reps	Weight/Resistance	Tempo	Time
1				30 sec

Mountain Climbers
1. Start by getting on your hands and feet in a prone position. {Push-up position)
2. Keeping your body parallel to the floor, drive your knees up towards your chest alternating back and forth.
3. Repeat this movement for the required number of seconds.

Additional Comments
Inform your athletes that this is similar to running in place with their hands on the floor. Make sure they are light on their feet in order to prevent ankle injury.

	Sets	Reps	Weight/Resistance	Tempo	Time
	1				15 sec R
	2				15 sec L

Single Leg Plank Raise
1. Start in a plank position (Push-up) then carefully lower your elbows and forearms to the floor.
2. Your body will remain parallel to the floor. .
3. Once the plank is formed raise one foot off the floor and then return to the starting position.
4. Repeat this movement for the desired repetitions.

Additional Comments
Perform Single Leg Plank Raise with one leg at a time.

Gymnastics Conditioning, Fitness Training
for the Gymnast

Sets	Reps	Weight/Resistance	Tempo	Time
				15 sec

Belly Blaster
1. Start in a plank position (Push-up) then carefully lower your elbows and forearms to the floor. Your body will remain parallel to the floor.
2. Pull your belly button in toward your spine and raise your hips up into the air.
3. Return to the starting and repeat for the prescribed number of repetitions.

Sets	Reps	Weight/Resistance	Tempo	Time
1		Floor		30 sec
2		Elevated		30 sec
3		Handstand		30 sec

Protraction / Shrugs
1. Start in a plank position (Push-up).
2. Your body will remain parallel to the floor.
3. Pull chest in and press up at the shoulders separating the shoulder blades and rounding the upper back.
5. Remember to keep the head and trunk stabilized in a neutral position by contracting the abdominal and back muscles. Avoid hyperextension of the low back and elbows.

Additional Comments
In order to tailor this to gymnastics, have your athletes keep their feet pointed. This will force them to keep their body tight while in motion. Also have your athletes move their arms further from their feet to perform more of a rainbow / hollow shape. Perform this exercise with feet elevated at 45 degrees and then in a handstand. Spot athletes for the handstand shrugs. See this drill in the book, "Gymnastics Drills and Conditioning for the Handstand."

Sets	Reps	Weight/Resistance	Tempo	Time
1		45 Degree		30 sec
2		Handstand		15 sec

Elevated and Handstand Pushup
1. Start by standing with your back facing the wall.
2. Next place your hands on the ground and then your feet on the wall so that you are a minimum of a 45 degree angle.
3. Proceed to bend your arms into a pushup position until you have reached your full range of motion.
4. Extend your arms and return to the starting position and repeat for the desired repetitions.
5. Make sure you have help from a coach.
6. Keep your head in a neutral position and your trunk stabilized by contracting the abdominal muscles. Avoid hyperextension of the low back and elbows.

Additional Comments
Have your gymnasts perform this exercise in a full handstand if they can remain tight. Spot them for the handstand push ups.

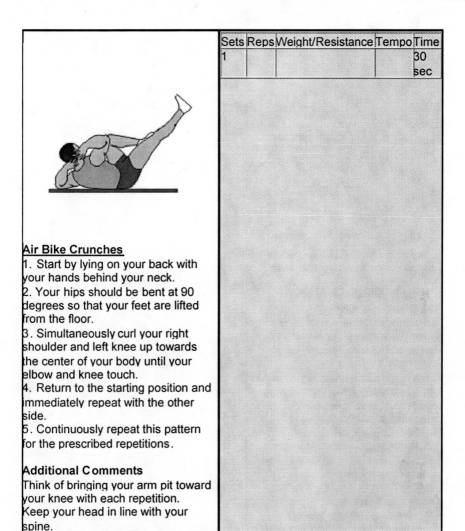

Sets	Reps	Weight/Resistance	Tempo	Time
1				30 sec

Air Bike Crunches

1. Start by lying on your back with your hands behind your neck.
2. Your hips should be bent at 90 degrees so that your feet are lifted from the floor.
3. Simultaneously curl your right shoulder and left knee up towards the center of your body until your elbow and knee touch.
4. Return to the starting position and immediately repeat with the other side.
5. Continuously repeat this pattern for the prescribed repetitions.

Additional Comments

Think of bringing your arm pit toward your knee with each repetition.
Keep your head in line with your spine.

Sets	Reps	Weight/Resistance	Tempo	Time
1				30 sec

Reverse Crunch (Tuck)
1. Start by lying on your back with your hands behind or above your head.
2. Bend knees. Knees will remain bent throughout exercise.
3. Proceed to draw in your belly button toward your spine and lift both legs up at the same time towards your chest.
4. Once knees are lifted into chest as much as possible, the buttocks will slightly lift off the floor, making the athlete more round.
5. Return to the starting position and repeat making sure that you do not arch your back as you are lowering or raising your legs.

Additional Comments
After this exercise and before they stretch you should have them take a 1 minute water break.

Core Training

Sets	Reps	Weight/ Resistance	Tempo	Time
1	10			
2	10			

Reverse Crunch (Tuck)

1. Start by lying on your back with your hands behind your head.
2. Bend knees. Knees will remain bent throughout exercise.
3. Proceed to draw in your belly button toward your spine and lift legs up at the same time towards chest.
4. Once knees are lifted into chest as much as possible, the buttocks will slightly lift off the floor, making the athlete more round.
5. Return to the starting position and repeat making sure that you do not arch your back as you are lowering or raising your legs.

Additional Comments

Alternate with Stick Crunch and Double Crunch. No rest between exercises.
Ten Reverse Crunches, Ten Stick Crunches, Ten Double Crunches.
All 3 exercises equal one round. Go through the combination twice for a total of 60 repetitions nonstop.

Sets	Reps	Weight/ Resistance	Tempo	Time
1	10			
2	10			

Stick Crunch
1. Start by lying on your back with your legs bent to 90 degrees.
2. Holding a stick, broom handle, or towel with both hands reach up and crunch towards your feet.
3. Slowly return to the starting position and repeat for the desired repetitions.

Trainer's comments:
Alternate with Reverse Crunch and Double Crunch. No rest between exercises.
Ten Reverse Crunches, Ten Stick Crunches, Ten Double Crunches.
All 3 exercises equal one round. Go through the combination twice for a total of 60 repetitions nonstop.

Sets	Reps	Weight/ Resistance	Tempo	Time
1	10			
2	10			

Double Crunch

1. Start by lying on your back with your hands behind your head or neck.
2. Keep elbows back and out of sight.
3. Bend your knees at 90 degrees.
4. Leading with the chin and chest toward the ceiling, contract your abdominals and raise your shoulders off the floor or bench.
5. As you lift your upper body, also bring your knees toward your chest.
6. Return to the starting position.
7. Remember to keep head and neck in a neutral position. Hyperextension or flexion of either can cause injury.

Additional comments

Alternate with Reverse Crunch and Stick Crunch. No rest between exercises.
Ten Reverse Crunches, Ten Stick Crunches, Ten Double Crunches.
All 3 exercises equal one round. Go through the combination twice for a total of 60 repetitions nonstop.

Sets	Reps	Weight/ Resistance	Tempo	Time
1	10			
2	10			

Air Bike Crunches

1. Start by lying on your back with your hands behind your neck.
2. Your hips should be bent at 90 degrees so that your feet are lifted from the floor.
3. Simultaneously curl your right shoulder and left knee up towards the center of your body until your elbow and knee touch.
4. Return to the starting position and immediately repeat with the other side.
5. Continuously repeat this pattern for the prescribed repetitions.

Additional Comments

Think of bringing your arm pit toward your knee with each repetition.
Keep your head in line with your spine.
Alternate with V-Up and Unilateral Leg Raise. No rest between exercises. Ten Bike Crunches, Ten V-Ups, Ten Unilateral Leg Raises. All 3 exercises equal one round. Go through the combination twice for a total of 60 repetitions nonstop.

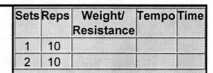

Sets	Reps	Weight/ Resistance	Tempo	Time
1	10			
2	10			

V-Up

1. Lie on back on floor with knees straight and arms extended so they are next to the ears.
2. Head should be in a neutral position with a space between chin and chest.
3. Leading with the chin and chest towards the ceiling, contract the abdominal muscles and raise shoulders and legs off floor.
4. Body will form a pike position, appearing as if it is folded ion half balancing on the buttocks.
5. Return to starting position and repeat.

Additional Comments

Athlete will attempt to touch hands to feet at top of exercise.
Alternate with Bike Crunch and Unilateral Leg Raise. No rest between exercises.
Ten Bike Crunches, Ten V-Ups, Ten Unilateral Leg Raises.
All 3 exercises equal one round. Go through the combination twice for a total of 60 repetitions nonstop.

Sets	Reps	Weight/ Resistance	Tempo	Time
1	10			
2	10			

Unilateral Leg Raise
1. Lie back on floor on top of a balance disc with both knees bent and feet flat. Place hands at sides.
2. Contract abdominal muscles continuously to stabilize your trunk.
3. Lower back should be in a neutral position.
4. Straighten both legs so that they are perpendicular to floor and your feet are pointed toward the ceiling.
5. Slowly lower one leg to approximately 45 degrees.
6. Bring that leg back up so the legs are together and perpendicular to the floor.
7. Next lower the other leg to approximately 45 degrees and bring it back up so the legs are together again.
8. Continue to lower and raise one leg at a time.

Additional Comments
Remember to maintain stability in lower back throughout movement by keeping abdominal muscles contracted. DO NOT ARCH LOWER BACK.
To increase intensity, lower legs past 45° without touching floor as long as

Core Training

trunk stability is maintained. **Alternate** with Bike Crunch and V-Up. No rest between exercises. Ten Bike Crunches, Ten V-Ups, Ten Unilateral Leg Raises. All 3 exercises equal one round. Go through the combination twice for a total of 60 repetitions nonstop.	

Sets	Reps	Weight/ Resistance	Tempo	Time
1	10			
2	10			

Straight Leg Modified Crunch (Hollow Body Lift)

1. Lie on back on floor or bench with your knees straight.
2. Place both hands on the front of your thighs, near hips.
3. Keep your head in a neutral position with a space between chin and chest throughout this exercise.
4. Leading with your chin and chest toward the ceiling, contract your abdominal muscles and raise your shoulders off the floor or bench.
5. Keeping your arms extended throughout this exercise, they should slide down your thighs as you lift your shoulder blades from the floor.
6. Return to start position.

Additional Comments

Remember to keep head and back in a neutral position. Hyperextension or flexion may cause injury.
Only curl your torso until your shoulders blades are off the floor.
Your lower back remains on the floor.
Do not try to sit up to an upright position.
For gymnastics, a hollow position is the goal on each lift. Your legs remain straight and feet pointed.

Core Training

Alternate with Ankle Wiggles and Hip Thrusts. No rest between exercises. Ten Straight Leg Crunch, Ten Ankle Wiggles, Ten Hip Thrusts. All 3 exercises equal one round. Go through the combination twice for a total of 60 repetitions nonstop.	

Gymnastics Conditioning, Fitness Training for the Gymnast

Gymnastics Conditioning, Fitness Training for the Gymnast

Sets	Reps	Weight/ Resistance	Tempo	Time
1	10			
2	10			

Ankle Wiggles
1. Lie on back on mat or bench with knees bent and hands at your side.
2. Your head should be in a neutral position with a space between your chin and chest.
3. Leading with the chin and chest towards the ceiling, contract the abdominal muscles and raise your shoulders off the mat or bench.
4. Reach for your ankle with one hand and then reach for the other ankle with your other hand.
5. Return to the starting position.
6. Remember to keep your head in a neutral position to prevent injury.

Additional Comments
Your low back remains on the floor throughout the exercise. This is a rocking side to side motion.
Alternate with Straight Leg Crunch and Hip Thrusts. No rest between exercises.
Ten Straight Leg Crunch, Ten Ankle Wiggles, Ten Hip Thrusts.
All 3 exercises equal one round. Go through the combination twice for a total of 60 repetitions nonstop.

Sets	Reps	Weight/ Resistance	Tempo	Time
1	10			
2	10			

Hip Thrusts
1. Lie on your back with your legs bent 90 degrees at the hip.
2. Your legs should be nearly straight.
3. Place your hands at your sides or behind your neck.
4. Slowly lift your hips off the floor and towards the ceiling.
5. Lower your hips to the floor and repeat for the prescribed number of repetitions.

Additional Comments
Alternate with Straight Arm/Leg Crunch and Ankle Wiggles. No rest between exercises. Ten Straight Leg Crunch, Ten Ankle Wiggles, Ten Hip Thrusts.
All 3 exercises equal one round. Go through the combination twice for a total of 60 repetitions nonstop.

	Sets	Reps	Weight/ Resistance	Tempo	Time
	1	10			

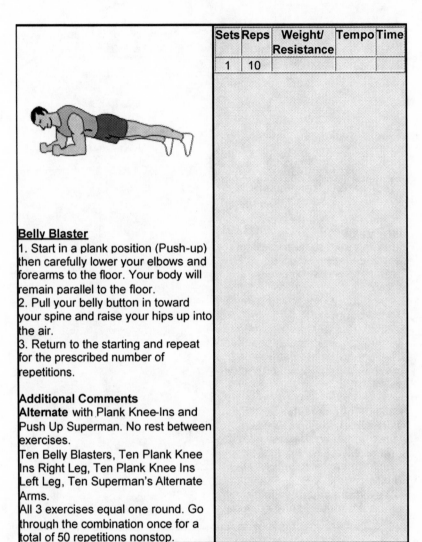

Belly Blaster
1. Start in a plank position (Push-up) then carefully lower your elbows and forearms to the floor. Your body will remain parallel to the floor.
2. Pull your belly button in toward your spine and raise your hips up into the air.
3. Return to the starting and repeat for the prescribed number of repetitions.

Additional Comments
Alternate with Plank Knee-Ins and Push Up Superman. No rest between exercises.
Ten Belly Blasters, Ten Plank Knee Ins Right Leg, Ten Plank Knee Ins Left Leg, Ten Superman's Alternate Arms.
All 3 exercises equal one round. Go through the combination once for a total of 50 repetitions nonstop.

Sets	Reps	Weight/ Resistance	Tempo	Time
1	10 Right			
2	10 Left			

Plank Knee-ins
1. Start in a plank position (Push-up).
2. Keeping your abdominal muscles tight and your trunk parallel bring one knee in toward your chest.
3. Do not allow your foot to touch the floor during the movement in or out.
3. Return your foot back to the starting position and repeat with the other leg.

Additional Comments
Alternate with Plank Knee-Ins.
Ten Belly Blasters, Ten Plank Knee-Ins with Right, Ten Plank Knee-Ins with Left.
Go through the combination once for a total of 30 repetitions nonstop.

Sets	Reps	Weight/ Resistance	Tempo	Time
1	10 Right			
2	10 Left			

Pushup Superman (Alternate Arms)

1. Start in a plank position (Push-up).
2. Holding that position raise your right arm and left leg off of the floor.
3. Return to the starting position and repeat with the left arm and right leg.
4. Hold each lift for 1-2 seconds.

Additional Comments

Alternate with Belly Blasters and Plank Knee-Ins. No rest between exercises.

Ten Belly Blasters, Ten Plank Knee Ins Right Leg, Ten Plank Knee Ins Left Leg, Ten Superman's Alternate Arms.

All 3 exercises equal one round. Go through the combination once for a total of 50 repetitions nonstop.

Sets	Reps	Weight/ Resistance	Tempo	Time
1	5			
2	5			

Hanging Hip Raise
(Tuck Leg Lifts)
1. Grab onto bar and hang from the bar in a relaxed and straight position.
2. Bring your knees up toward your chest, going at least as high as your hips.
3. Keeping your back firmly pressed against back support, slowly lower legs to the start position.
4. Continue to lift and lower your legs for the prescribed number of repetitions.
4. Remember to keep your head and neck in a neutral position.
5. Keep your abdominal muscles tight (naval drawn in towards spine) throughout the entire movement.

Additional Comments
Keep your feet pointed. This exercise is most efficient if a coach holds the athlete's back to prevent swinging.
Alternate with Straight Leg Lifts.
Ten Tuck Leg Lifts, Ten Straight Leg Lifts. No rest between exercises.
Both exercises equal one round.
Go through the combination twice for a total of 20 repetitions nonstop.

Sets	Reps	Weight/ Resistance	Tempo	Time
1	5			
2	5			

Leg Raise
(Pike Leg Lift)
1. Grab onto bar and hang from the bar in a relaxed and straight position.
2. Proceed to raise your legs up and touch your feet to the bar.
3. Keep legs as straight throughout the exercise.
4. Do not swing during this motion.
5. Return to the starting position and repeat.

Additional Comments
Keep head neutral. Your arms remain in line with your ears. Keep legs straight and feet pointed. This exercise is most efficient if a coach holds the athlete's back to prevent swinging.
Alternate with Tuck Leg Lifts.
Ten Tuck Leg Lifts, Ten Straight Leg Lifts.
No rest between exercises. Both exercises equal one round. Go through the combination twice for a total of 20 repetitions nonstop.

Core Training 2nd Workout

Sets	Reps	Weight/ Resistance	Tempo	Time
1	10			
2	10			

Reverse Crunch (Tuck)
1. Lie on your back with your hands behind your head.
2. Bend knees. Knees will remain bent throughout exercise.
3. Draw in your belly button toward your spine and lift both legs up towards your chest.
4. Once knees are lifted into chest as much as possible, the buttocks will slightly lift off the floor, making the athlete more round.
5. Return to the starting position and repeat making sure that you do not arch your back as you are lowering or raising your legs.

Additional Comments
Alternate with Double Crunch and Bike Crunch. No rest between exercises.
Ten Reverse Crunches, Ten Double Crunches, Ten Bike Crunches.
All 3 exercises equal one round. Go through the combination twice for a total of 60 repetitions nonstop.

Sets	Reps	Weight/ Resistance	Tempo	Time
1	10			
2	10			

Double Crunch
1. Start by lying on your back with your hands behind your head or neck.
2. Keep elbows back and out of sight.
3. Bend your knees at 90 degrees.
4. Leading with the chin and chest toward the ceiling, contract your abdominals and raise your shoulders off the floor or bench.
5. As you lift your upper body, also bring your knees toward your chest.
6. Return to the starting position.
7. Remember to keep head and neck in a neutral position. Hyperextension or flexion of either can cause injury.

Additional comments
Alternate with Reverse Crunch and Bike Crunch. No rest between exercises.
Ten Reverse Crunches, Ten Double Crunches, Ten Bike Crunches.
All 3 exercises equal one round. Go through the combination twice for a total of 60 repetitions nonstop.

Sets	Reps	Weight/ Resistance	Tempo	Time
1	10			
2	10			

Air Bike Crunches
1. Start by lying on your back with your hands behind your neck.
2. Your hips should be bent at 90 degrees so that your feet are lifted from the floor.
3. Simultaneously curl your right shoulder and left knee up towards the center of your body until your elbow and knee touch.
4. Return to the starting position and immediately repeat with the other side.
5. Continuously repeat this pattern for the prescribed repetitions.

Additional Comments
Think of bringing your arm pit toward your knee with each repetition.
Keep your head in line with your spine.
Alternate with Reverse Crunch and Double Crunch. No rest between exercises.
Ten Reverse Crunches, Ten Double Crunches, Ten Bike Crunches.
All 3 exercises equal one round. Go through the combination twice for a total of 60 repetitions nonstop.

Gymnastics Conditioning, Fitness Training for the Gymnast

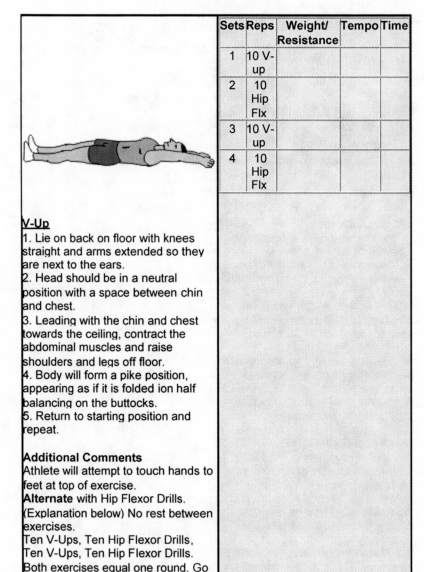

Sets	Reps	Weight/ Resistance	Tempo	Time
1	10 V-up			
2	10 Hip Flx			
3	10 V-up			
4	10 Hip Flx			

V-Up
1. Lie on back on floor with knees straight and arms extended so they are next to the ears.
2. Head should be in a neutral position with a space between chin and chest.
3. Leading with the chin and chest towards the ceiling, contract the abdominal muscles and raise shoulders and legs off floor.
4. Body will form a pike position, appearing as if it is folded ion half balancing on the buttocks.
5. Return to starting position and repeat.

Additional Comments
Athlete will attempt to touch hands to feet at top of exercise.
Alternate with Hip Flexor Drills.
(Explanation below) No rest between exercises.
Ten V-Ups, Ten Hip Flexor Drills, Ten V-Ups, Ten Hip Flexor Drills. Both exercises equal one round. Go through the combination twice, nonstop for a total of 40 repetitions.

HIP FLEXOR DRILL
1. Sit on floor in pike position, legs

straight in front of body and together.
2. Place hands on floor next to knees.
3. Keeping legs straight, feet pointed, buttocks on floor lift both legs to shoulder height and lower.
4. Repeat several times quickly.
5. As the gymnast gains strength in the hip flexor, the hands can be placed further from the body, closer to ankles. Illustrations found in book, "Gymnastics Drills and Conditioning Exercises."
ISBN: 9781411605794

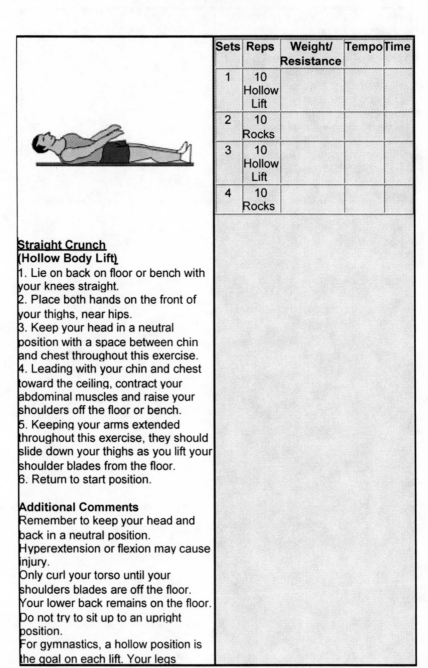

	Sets	Reps	Weight/ Resistance	Tempo	Time
	1	10 Hollow Lift			
	2	10 Rocks			
	3	10 Hollow Lift			
	4	10 Rocks			

Straight Crunch
(Hollow Body Lift)
1. Lie on back on floor or bench with your knees straight.
2. Place both hands on the front of your thighs, near hips.
3. Keep your head in a neutral position with a space between chin and chest throughout this exercise.
4. Leading with your chin and chest toward the ceiling, contract your abdominal muscles and raise your shoulders off the floor or bench.
5. Keeping your arms extended throughout this exercise, they should slide down your thighs as you lift your shoulder blades from the floor.
6. Return to start position.

Additional Comments
Remember to keep your head and back in a neutral position.
Hyperextension or flexion may cause injury.
Only curl your torso until your shoulders blades are off the floor.
Your lower back remains on the floor.
Do not try to sit up to an upright position.
For gymnastics, a hollow position is the goal on each lift. Your legs

remain straight and feet pointed.
Alternate with Hollow Rocks.
(Explained below.)
No rest between exercises.
Ten Straight Leg Crunch, Ten Hollow Rocks, Ten Straight Leg Crunch, Ten Hollow Rocks. Go through the combination twice for a total of 40 repetitions nonstop

HOLLOW ROCKS
1. Same starting position as above.
2. Once head and shoulder blades are off floor, lift heels off floor to initiate rocking motion.
3. Rocking motion can be maintained by contracting abdominal muscles, alternating the upper and lower abdominal contraction.
4. Remain hollow throughout exercise.
5. Think of the bottom of a rocking chair, remain curved and alternate the up and down motion.

Sets	Reps	Weight/ Resistance	Tempo	Time
1	10			
2	10			

Hip Thrusts
1. Lie on your back with your legs bent 90 degrees at the hip.
2. Your legs should be nearly straight.
3. Place your hands at your sides or behind your neck.
4. Slowly lift your hips off the floor and towards the ceiling.
5. Lower your hips to the floor and repeat for the prescribed number of repetitions.

Additional Comments
Alternate with Alternating Toe Touch and Leg Raise. No rest between exercises. Ten Hip Thrusts, Ten Alternating Toe Touch, Ten Leg Raises.
All 3 exercises equal one round. Go through the combination twice for a total of 60 repetitions nonstop.

Sets	Reps	Weight/ Resistance	Tempo	Time
1	10			
2	10			

Alternating Toe Touch
1. Lie on back on floor or bench.
2. Raise feet up into the air.
3. Your legs should be nearly straight.
3. Your head should be in a neutral position with a space between chin and chest.
4. Leading with your chin and chest toward the ceiling, contract the abdominal and raise your shoulders off the floor or bench.
5. Extend one arm and reach for the opposite foot.
6. Return to starting position and repeat with other hand.
7. Remember to keep your head and back in a neutral position. Hyperextension or flexion may cause injury.

Additional Comments
Alternate with Hip Thrusts and Leg Raises. No rest between exercises. Ten Hip Thrusts, Ten Alternating Toe Touches, Ten Leg Raises.
All 3 exercises equal one round. Go through the combination twice for a total of 60 repetitions nonstop.

Sets	Reps	Weight/ Resistance	Tempo	Time
1	10			
2	10			

Leg Raise
1. Start by lying on your back with a slight bend in your knees.
2. Raise your legs to a perpendicular position to the floor. Feet should be pointing toward the ceiling. This is your starting position.
3. Slowly lower your legs until you are no longer able to keep your abdominal muscles tight.
4. If your lower back begins to lift off the floor stop lowering your legs. Keep your lower back on the floor.
5. Raise your legs back up to the starting position and repeat.

Additional Comments
Alternate with Hip Thrusts and Alternating Toe Touch. No rest between exercises.
Ten Hip Thrusts, Ten Alternating Toe Touches, Ten Leg Raises.
All 3 exercises equal one round. Go through the combination twice for a total of 60 repetitions nonstop.

Core and Upper Body

Sets	Reps	Weight/ Resistance	Tempo	Time
1	10			
2	10			

Stick Crunch
1. Start by lying on your back with your legs bent to 90 degrees.
2. Holding a stick, broom handle, or towel with both hands reach up and crunch towards your feet.
3. Slowly return to the starting position and repeat for the desired repetitions.

Additional Comments:
Alternate with Double Crunch and Reverse Crunch. No rest between exercises.
10 Stick Crunches, 10 Double Crunches, 10 Reverse Crunches.
Go through all 3 exercises twice for a total of 60 repetitions.

Sets	Reps	Weight/ Resistance	Tempo	Time
1	10			
2	10			

Double Crunch
1. Start by lying on your back with your hands behind your head or neck.
2. Keep elbows back and out of sight.
3. Bend your knees at 90 degrees.
4. Leading with the chin and chest toward the ceiling, contract your abdominals and raise your shoulders off the floor or bench.
5. As you lift your upper body, also bring your knees toward your chest.
6. Return to the starting position.
7. Remember to keep head and neck in a neutral position. Hyperextension or flexion of either can cause injury.

Additional comments
Alternate with Stick Crunch and Reverse Crunch. No rest between exercises.
Ten Stick Crunches, Ten Double Crunches, Ten Reverse Crunches. All 3 exercises equal one round. Go through the combination twice for a total of 60 repetitions.

Sets	Reps	Weight/ Resistance	Tempo	Time
1	10			
2	10			

Reverse Crunch

1. Start by lying on your back with your hands behind or above your head.
2. Bend knees. Knees will remain bent throughout exercise.
3. Proceed to draw in your belly button toward your spine and lift both legs up at the same time towards your chest.
4. Once knees are lifted into chest as much as possible, the buttocks will slightly lift off the floor, making the athlete more round.
5. Return to the starting position and repeat making sure that you do not arch your back as you are lowering or raising your legs.

Additional Comments

This exercise should be alternated with Stick Crunch and Double Crunch.
Ten Stick Crunch, Ten Double Crunch, Ten Reverse Crunch. Go through all 3 exercises twice for a total of 60 repetitions.

	Sets	Reps	Weight/ Resistance	Tempo	Time
	1	10			
	2	10			
	3	10			
	4	10			

Oblique Crunch

1. Start by placing your left foot over your right knee and place your hands behind your head or neck.
2. Lift your shoulders up off the floor and twist so that your right elbow moves toward your left knee.
3. Return to the starting position and repeat the required number of repetitions.
4. Repeat with the other side.

Additional Comments

This exercise should be alternated with Air Bike Crunches. No rest between exercises.
Ten Oblique Crunches-Right, Ten Oblique Crunches-Left, Ten Bike Crunches.
Go through the combination twice for a total of 60 repetitions nonstop

Sets	Reps	Weight/ Resistance	Tempo	Time
1	10			
2	10			
3	10			
4	10			

Air Bike Crunches
1. Start by lying on your back with your hands behind your neck.
2. Your hips should be bent at 90 degrees so that your feet are lifted from the floor.
3. Simultaneously curl your right shoulder and left knee up towards the center of your body until your elbow and knee touch.
4. Return to the starting position and immediately repeat with the other side.
5. Continuously repeat this pattern for the prescribed repetitions.

Additional Comments
Think of bringing your arm pit toward your knee with each repetition.
Keep your head in line with your spine.
Alternate with Oblique Crunches. No rest between exercises.
Ten Oblique Crunches-Right, Ten Oblique Crunches-Left, Ten Bike Crunches.
Go through the combination twice for a total of 60 repetitions nonstop

Sets	Reps	Weight/ Resistance	Tempo	Time
1	10			
2	10			
3	10			
4	10			

Unilateral Leg Raise
1 Lie back on floor on top of a balance disc with both knees bent and feet flat. Place hands at sides.
2. Contract abdominal muscles continuously to stabilize your trunk.
3. Lower back should be in a neutral position.
4. Straighten both legs so that they are perpendicular to floor and your feet are pointed toward the ceiling.
5. Slowly lower one leg to approximately 45 degrees.
6. Bring that leg back up so the legs are together and perpendicular to the floor.
7. Next lower the other leg to approximately 45 degrees and bring it back up so the legs are together again.
8. Continue to lower and raise one leg at a time.

Additional Comments
Remember to maintain stability in lower back throughout movement by keeping abdominal muscles contracted. DO NOT ARCH LOWER BACK.
To increase intensity, lower legs past 45° without touching floor as long as

trunk stability is maintained.
Alternate with Hip Thrusts. No rest
between exercises.
Ten Unilateral Leg Raises (Both),
Ten Hip Thrusts, Ten Unilateral Leg
Raises (Both). Ten Hip Thrusts
Go through both exercises twice for a
total of 60 repetitions.

Sets	Reps	Weight/ Resistance	Tempo	Time
1	10			
2	10			

Hip Thrusts
1. Lie on your back with your legs bent 90 degrees at the hip.
2. Your legs should be nearly straight.
3. Place your hands at your sides or behind your neck.
4. Slowly lift your hips off the floor and towards the ceiling.
5. Lower your hips to the floor and repeat for the prescribed number of repetitions.

Additional Comments
Alternate with Unilateral Leg Raise.
No rest between exercises.
Ten Unilateral Leg Raises (Both), Ten Hip Thrusts, Ten Unilateral Leg Raises (Both). Ten Hip Thrusts
Go through both exercises twice for a total of 60 repetitions.

Sets	Reps	Weight/ Resistance	Tempo	Time
1	15			
2	15			

Protraction / Shrugs

1. Lie face down on the floor with hands palm down, fingers pointing straight ahead, and aligned at the nipple line.
2. Place hands shoulder width, and feet should be at hip width with toes on floor.
3. Extend the elbows and raise the body off the floor.
4. Extend at the elbows and pressing up at the shoulders separating the shoulder blades and arching the upper back.
5. Remember to keep the head and trunk stabilized in a neutral position by contracting the abdominal and back muscles. Avoid hyperextension of the low back and elbows.

Additional Comments

In order to tailor this to gymnastics, have your athletes keep their feet pointed. This will force them to keep their body tight while in motion. Also have your athletes move their arms further from their feet to perform more of a rainbow / hollow shape. Perform this exercise with feet elevated at 45 degrees and then in a handstand. Spot athletes for the handstand shrugs. See this drill in the book, "Gymnastics Drills and Conditioning for the Handstand."

Alternate with Explosive Push Up.
No rest between exercises.
Fifteen Protractions, Fifteen Explosive Push Ups, Fifteen Protractions), Fifteen Explosive Push Ups.
Elevate Feet Fifteen Protractions, Fifteen Explosive Push Ups.
Elevate Feet for second set of Protractions, but not for Explosive Push Ups.

Sets	Reps	Weight/ Resistance	Tempo	Time
1	15			
2	15			

Explosive Pushup
1. Start by getting into a push-up position.
2. Lower yourself to the floor and then explosively push up so that your hands leave the floor.
3. Catch your fall with your hands and immediately bend your arms, lowering yourself back to the floor.
4. Repeat for the recommended repetitions.
5. Keep your head and trunk stabilized in a neutral position by contracting the abdominal muscles. Avoid arching the low back.

Additional Comments
Alternate with Protractions.
No rest between exercises.
Fifteen Protractions, Fifteen Explosive Push Ups, Fifteen Protractions), Fifteen Explosive Push Ups.
Elevate Feet Fifteen Protractions, Fifteen Explosive Push Ups.
Elevate Feet for second set of Protractions, but not for Explosive Push Ups.

Sets	Reps	Weight/ Resistance	Tempo	Time
1	15 at 45 Degree			
2	15 Handstand			

Elevated and Handstand Push-up

1. Start by standing with your back facing the wall.
2. Next place your hands on the ground and then your feet on the wall so that you are a minimum of a 45 degree angle.
3. Proceed to bend your arms into a pushup position until you have reached your full range of motion.
4. Extend your arms and return to the starting position and repeat for the desired repetitions.
5. Make sure you have help from a coach.
6. Keep your head in a neutral position and your trunk stabilized by contracting the abdominal muscles. Avoid hyperextension of the low back and elbows.

Additional Comments

Have your gymnasts perform this exercise in a full handstand if they can remain tight. Spot them for the handstand push ups.

Sets	Reps	Weight/ Resistance	Tempo	Time
1	15			
2	15			

Dive Bomber Pushup

1. Lie face down on the floor with hands palm down, fingers pointing straight ahead, and aligned at the nipple line.
2. Place hands slightly wider than shoulder width.
3. Feet should be at hip width with toes on floor.
4. Extend the elbows and raise the body off the floor.
5. Move your feet in so that your buttocks is higher than your shoulders.
6. Lower one section of your body a time 4-8 inches from the floor starting with the head first and follow with the shoulders and waist.
6. It should look like you are diving down toward the floor.
7. Return to the start position by extending at the elbows and pushing the body up.
8. Remember to keep the head and trunk stabilized in a neutral position by contracting the abdominal and back muscles.

Additional Comments

Never fully lock the elbows at the start position and avoid hyperextension of the low back. Do not hit your head or scrape your face during this exercise.

	Sets	Reps	Weight/ Resistance	Tempo	Time
	1	15			
	2	15			

Prone Knee Tuck on ball
1. Start in a push up position with your feet on top of a stability ball.
2. Slowly bring your knees in toward your chest and then return to the starting position.
3. As your knees crunch in your hips will rise. Do not allow your hands to move.
3. When your legs are extended make sure to keep your hips parallel with your body and do not let them sag toward the floor.

Additional Comments
An octagon or barrel mat can be used. At the top of the exercise pull your head in line with her arms to simulate a handstand. Try to position your buttocks above your head at the top of the exercise to simulate a handstand. Think of a cast to handstand on uneven bars while performing this exercise.

About Author

Karen Goeller is the author of the famous gymnastics drills and conditioning books. She has been a fitness trainer over 15 years and a gymnastics coach for 25. She has had gymnastics articles published in Technique Magazine and on various gymnastics websites.

Before her success as a published author, Karen owned and operated a gymnastics club
in NYC for 10 years, worked for the most famous gymnastics coach, Bela Karolyi for seven summers, worked at International Gymnastics Camp for a decade of holiday clinics, and worked at various health clubs in NYC.

Before Karen earned her BA Degree, her studies included Physical Therapy, Health Sciences, Nutrition, and Emergency Medical Care. She has held certifications such as NYS EMT, Nutritional Analysis, Fitness Trainer, USA Gymnastics Safety, Skill Evaluator, and Meet Director among many others.

More recently Karen has become a Proctor and Teacher for the Fitness Trainer Certification Exam.

Other Books by this Author

Gymnastics Drills and Conditioning Exercises
ISBN: 978-1-4116-0579-4

Gymnastics Drills and Conditioning for the Handstand
ISBN: 978-1-4116-5000-8

Gymnastics Drills... Walkover, Limber, and Back Handspring
ISBN: 978-1-4116-1160-3

Gymnastics Conditioning for the Legs and Ankles
ISBN: 978-1-4116-2033-9

Gymnastics Journal... My Scores, My Goals, My Dreams
ISBN: 978-1-4116-4145-7

The Most Frequently Asked Questions about Gymnastics
ISBN: 1-59113-372-6

Fitness Journal: My Goals, My Training, and My Success
ISBN: 978- -1-84728-444-0

Strength Journal
ISBN: Not yet assigned.

Gymnastics Conditioning: Tumbling Conditioning
E-Book

Fitness Program: Strength Training and Core Workout
E-Book

Fitness Program: General Conditioning with Dumbbells
E-Book

Fitness Program: Dumbbells and Fitness Ball
E-Book

www.GymnasticsDrills.com

Safety Warning

These workouts have been designed for Level 6 Gymnasts and up.

Please keep in mind that you are responsible for the safety of your gymnasts and / or yourself. By completing this workout with your athletes you assume the responsibility for your athletes and / or yourself.

WARNING: Any activity involving motion or height creates the possibility of accidental injury, paralysis or death.
The equipment and instructional materials are intended for use ONLY by properly trained and qualified participants under supervised conditions. Use without proper supervision could be DANGEROUS and should NOT be undertaken or permitted. Before using, KNOW YOUR OWN LIMITATIONS and the limitations of the equipment. If in doubt always consult your instructor. Always inspect equipment for loose fittings or damage and test for stability before each use.

We will not be liable for injuries or consequences sustained in the use of the instructional materials, supplies, or equipment sold by us.

Printed in the United States
114487LV00005B/192/A